verdure

KYLIE LITTEL

Interior Design by FormattedBooks.com

ISBN: 979-8-88589-597-2

Verdure [ver-dure \'vər-jər]
(noun)

new green vegetation,

growth.

CONTENTS

AUTHOR'S NOTE

I've tried to type this page many times over the last 3 years that this book has been in progress. I don't think a single word in here is the same as the ones in its beginning, but I think that's what growth looks like. Scrapping what we swore to be true, and replacing it with a fresher, more grown version. After many seasons of change, and many versions of me, I think I've finally landed upon a revised image of myself that can flourish and bloom.

These words bound between these pages felt like a safe place, a space for my mind to be free, but they don't do much good hiding in my notebook. Writing these words helped me grow and helped me find who I am, and who I want to be. I guarantee there are errors in these pages, no matter how hard I try to fight them. But I'm certainly not perfect, so I decided my book doesn't have to be, either. So, here's my heart, masquerading as book pages, and I hope your heart can relate to something in here, too.

Here's to growth,
here's to verdure.

All the Atoms in the Sky

The atmosphere is crafted of atoms.
Nitrogen, oxygen, carbon, argon, and some others
that are in such minuscule quantities
that we write them off as only trace amounts.

The universe is composed of stars, about as many
as atoms in the air, but the only ones visible to us
have lived their existence and spend the rest of eternity
sedentary in the exosphere.

The earth is much more minute than we'd like to believe.
But we, much like atoms in the atmosphere,
and stars in the Milky Way,
make up its inhabitance and believe
we play some bigger part
in this arbitrary picture painted
with someone else's hand.

And so, if there can be that many atoms in the ether,
and that multitude of stars in the galaxy,
I hope somewhere within this
inconsequential population of life,
there is someone that can make this
world feel a little smaller,

a little calmer,

a little lighter.

And can make me feel like I'm made
of whimsy and stardust,
and not just a makeshift composition
of all the atoms in the sky.

A Garden of Empty Promises

He opened the gate around my heart
like he owned it,
and started to water the deeply embedded roots of
past hurt like he was going to salvage
any of the remaining buds.

He was determined to make use of my scars like plots to
produce new fruit. Fruit less sour,
less bitter, less resentful.

He talked about marrying me like next
seasons harvest was a given,
and like those words didn't carry any weight.

This wasn't the first time a man had sung this tune,
promising me the world as I knew it. But I'm smarter now.
I know such proclamations never
hold up their end up the deal.

I've learned how to tend to my own needs,
and I will reap and sow this dirt,
a seed planted for every man that
makes me a chimeric declaration to stay.
And in time I'll have a garden.

I'll have a garden full of empty promises
from men who always take my flowers and leave me
with nothing but weeds and futile words.

Never Will

You think you've grown out of it.
You've lived enough years between then and now,
and time has to heal every wound.
But they don't put a limit on how much time it takes.
How much time is needed to stitch up gashes that reopen
themselves every morning at dawn.

You think you've moved on.
You're 20 now and those feelings
belonged to a naïve 16-year-old girl.
A girl that never lost the hope that fate was real,
and that you only really love one person in your lifetime.
She was terrified she had already found the one.

You think it's all in the past.
But that past seems to be a broken record
that repeats the same knowledge that she knew then,
and knows now.
He never loved her.
Love is a 2-way street,
and he wasn't in the mood for a drive.

You think it's over now.
Until you're listening to those old songs,
in an old town that hasn't changed since its beginning,
holding on to feelings that haven't changed either.

But you know you have.
And he's changed too.

But there are just some things that

never will.

A City I Don't Know

It's a strange feeling, you know?
Going from living in the world behind someone's eyes,
to becoming nothing more than a tourist.
Only stopping to see the attractions
that drew people there in the first place.
The places you go in cities you don't know.

They're no longer your hometown,
the town that you knew without a doubt
 would be waiting for you to return someday.
Reliable.
The town that you discovered magic in all
the places that aren't on the map.
The dark alley ways,
and abandoned construction sites,
and ponds filled to the brim with algae.
The places that would make you run from that city
if you didn't love it so damn much.

You became a city I needed a GPS to navigate.
I didn't know the street signs or speed limits.
I couldn't tell you the nearest gas station or coffee shop.
I don't know any of the towns drama
because you stopped letting me in on that long ago.
You went from being a small town to feeling like
a city of a million in a matter of minutes
and I don't recognize any of the faces on these streets.

The streets that once
had a population of two
became that of one
with a one-way ticket
to a city I don't know.

50 in a 55

I have only ever requested the bare minimum.
Never asking for more,
because I didn't think I deserved it.

But maybe the minimum was never minimal.
Maybe it was always just someone that will go 50 in a 55
to hold your hand a little while longer.

Placeholder

The way I loved became a "before and after" you.
I have to question if my feelings for anyone else
are just a placeholder for the lifelessness you left in me.
Someone to make me feel anything for a moment.

Someone to take your spot for a while,
until I realize they just don't fit.
I'm a puzzle I can't finish because you will always be
the lost piece that I can't find
no matter how hard I look.

Even after all this time I somehow
still can't look at you without feeling the stitches snip
on wounds that weren't quite healed
just to be left with a sea of crimson
pouring out of my chest.

They become placeholders.
And I know that's not fair to them,
but how could it possibly be fair to me to
spend the rest of my dandelions and stars
wishing it could have been different?

You made me believe in love
and simultaneously made me deny its existence
because how can I always love more than I am loved
and believe in this arbitrary idea that leaves me with
placeholders that can never replace

you.

I Made a Friend

Today I decided I don't want to be my own
worst enemy.

I just want to be my friend.

Spread My Ashes in Venice, Please.

When I die, whether today, tomorrow,
or when decades have passed,
spread my ashes in Venice, please.

I've never been there, but I hope to
see it before my body is
no more than a mere pile of dust.

I've never seen the colors dripping from the windowsills
and the rivers running like veins
through the heart of the city.
But somehow, I know it's where I was always meant to be.

And I know my soul never belonged here,
in the place that dusk meets me at 4pm
in our favorite driveway to watch the sunset.

My soul never belonged here,
in the place that meadow flowers aren't accessible to me
when I need them most.

My soul never belonged here,
in the place that took my spirit and
ground it down to powder
almost as fine as what I'll inevitably become.

My soul never belonged here.
And I don't want my eternal resting place
to be the place I always wanted to escape.

So please, spread my ashes in Venice.
Maybe then I can finally feel at home.

Shooting Stars

I wished on a shooting star once,
and never told anyone what I wished for.

What I wanted more than anything
was to meet the love of my life.

I guess I should have been more specific
with that wish, because he did come.

But I had just assumed that the love of my life
would have loved me too.

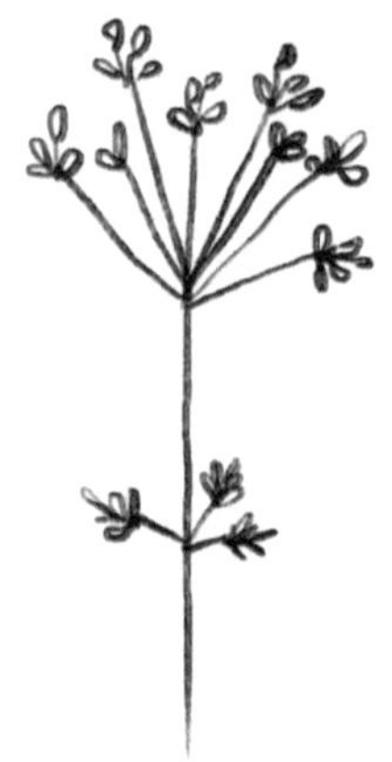

When Things Look Different

When I was little, we had Christmas on my mom's side on Christmas Eve, and we went to church every year and sat in the same row for as long as I can remember. I grew up going to this church, it hasn't changed since then, probably since long before then. We didn't miss a service, lighting candles for Silent Night. Except for the one time that my dad showed up drunk, and I said I was sick and went back to my grandma's house. First one I had missed in 20 years.

It was in that sanctuary that I learned who Jesus was, and who he wasn't. He wasn't like the rich white family that were always in the front row, singing, praying, and then scoffing at a homeless man on their way home. It was here that I learned who I didn't want to be.

Every year after service we would eat dinner, open gifts, and my 90-year-old grandpa would play me in checkers. He won every year, even when I tried, but this year he moved a piece too far and moved one the wrong way, but I didn't tell him, I let him win. Tradition after all, and I feared I wouldn't have many games left with him.

On Christmas Day, we saw my dad's side of the family. It had always been this way, and we opened up gifts one at a time in order of age. I was the youngest of the family, until my brother, so I always got to go first. We filled my grandmas small condo, played cards and dominos, like clockwork.

My cousins are all significantly older than me, married
with a lot (and I mean a lot) of kids. And most of them
started having Christmas on their own, doing their
own thing, and I haven't seen many of them in years.
This year, it was just my mom, dad, and brother there
on Christmas Day in my grandmas new apartment.

And someday, my grandma won't be there, my grandpa
won't be there, and I'll be left cherishing moments
that I never thought would slip out of grasp. I should
have held them tighter. Time trickles through and
changes things, but I didn't know it would be so soon.

Things may look different, but the memories are
still stitched into my brain like pictures in a scrap
book. And eventually, the people that were in the
very first pictures will be gone, and maybe I'll even
take on a similar role that my grandparents had.

I guess for now, I'll take photos, lots of them, of
all the moments I know I'll miss. I'll collect the
memories in trinkets that never seemed to be too
significant until the meaning attached was a person.
I'll remember hugs and hold them a bit longer.

I suppose it's just a fact of life, when things
look different is when you realize how
much you liked the way things were.

Pedestals

We spend so much time placing
people on pedestals that we forget,

we're worth something, too.

My Eyes are Turning Green

I have always had blue eyes.
Since the day I was born to after more
than 20 years have passed,
my eyes have resembled the ocean, or the sky,
or my polka dot rain boots.

My driver's license says my eyes are blue.
But today, I noticed that they are turning green.
And I'm not sure what that means for me,
because I have always identified as having blue eyes.

I have always had to be strong.
Since the day I was born to after more
than 20 years have passed,
my strength resembled that of graphene,
or of spider silk, or titanium.

My identity says that I am strong.
But today, I noticed that my legs can't always
hold me up, and my courage sometimes falls
short, and I don't always have it together.
And I'm not sure what this means for me,
because I have always identified as having strength.

I put myself in boxes labeled "blue eyes" and
"strong" and "resilient" and "fighter"
all without realizing that my identity,
just like my eyes, can change
with no control of my own.

My eyes are changing, and so am I. My identity is
changing, and so am I. I'm becoming a new version of me,

green eyes and all.

Inked

As I sit on the edge of this dock
under teardrop laden clouds,
I look into a lake so dark it's as if a
quill knocked over an ink jar
and splattered itself across the water.

You were like ink.

You were like a tattoo needle puncturing my skin,
leaving your mark all over me.

You were like a pen overflowing with
sentiments and apprehension,
guiding my hand across a contract signing
away the rights to my body.

You left me stained and interpreted it
as consent in a Rorschach test.

And now the water in front of me ripples
with the smallest droplet making its descent.

A miniscule amount of water,
but still adding to the vastness.

You were nothing more than a ripple in my life,
nothing more than a moment,

but you'll leave me permanently inked.

That Kind of Quiet

You rarely find that kind of quiet in the city.
The kind that echoes the chirp of the light rail,
or the kind that makes you notice the sound
of the snowflakes as they land on your jacket,
after cascading through the sky.

Silence, for me, is hard to come by.
The deafening dissonance of my own thoughts
leaves little room for anything other than
the occasional hush that is filled by the constant
ring in my ears anyway.

I've never known silence.
But I think today in this city, under a gray sky
that is still bright at 6:30pm,
this must be pretty close.
This must be what it's supposed to sound like.

Inspiration has been lacking as of late,
because my soul is too happy and
that's a contradictory statement
because "too" is underlined
with 2 blue lines wanting it to be replaced with
"so" or "very" because "too" isn't a word
that belongs in front of happy.

But it's true, I don't know how to write
without it being about desolation.
Because when that's all you have ever felt,
your mind finds a way to cope with that,
but it never learns now to feel anything else.

I think today I can see that
words don't always have to be melancholy.
And solitude isn't always isolation.
And sometimes a brief moment of calm
forces you to notice the rarity of
that kind of quiet,
nestled within the rumbling city.

Archive

I thought I wrote these words for someone to find.

But when I look back at them after a few years,

I see that I really wrote them for me to find again.

They become an archive of

who I was,

who I am,

and who I want to be.

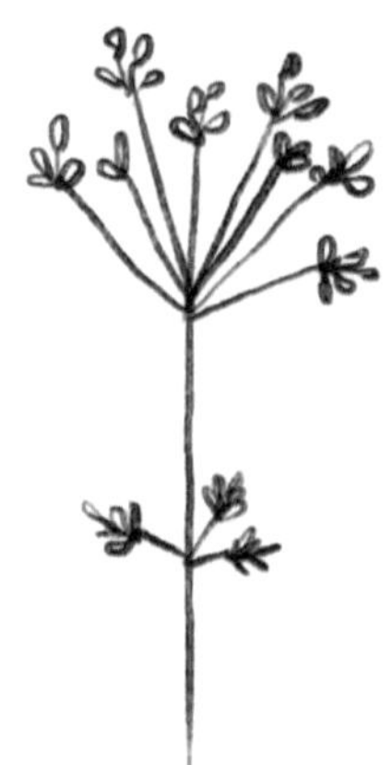

Talking to the Embers

It was 1:00 am on the warmest night of the year,
the noise had dulled,
and the fire smoldering.

I look around the circle
at all the first chance lovers that were filled with the hope
that this time might be different.

I knew it never would be.
I asked the embers when it would be my turn.
The white-hot charred wood never
gave me the answers I sought.

The dying ash looked like a freshly erupted volcano,
with lava seeping through every pore.
It resembled that of all the times my heart bled
for the ones who couldn't comprehend the flames
that rushed through my veins.

You can't control the fire.
You can't control who he loves, either.
All I could do is sit and ask the embers
when will my fire burn bright enough for him to see?

Be Alone

He told me some man would be very lucky to have me,
but it left me questioning why it couldn't be him.

I cut them out and run away and not one asked me to stay
and maybe that's ok because I don't
need a man to be lucky to have me.

I just want to be a little less afraid to

be alone.

Josephine St., CO, 80205

I had mostly assumed I would stay in one place.
Wandering far but coming back to the
comfort I'd always known.

In a residential neighborhood, on
Josephine St. of Denver,
I realized that the world is so much
bigger than we give it credit for.

There were beautiful houses with manicured
lawns, and dogs. So many dogs.
And kids running and playing without
ever having contact with reality.

There are coffee shops,
and horizons dotted with mountains,
and so much life left to be had.

Josephine St. looked like a hidden gem
that says if you keep going,
you'll find me again.
There was joy in this city,
and a peace in my heart.

There was somehow comfort in the unknown,
a realization of how far my wings can soar
if I release them to the wind.

I'll see you again, Josephine St., when time allows,
and my soul knows it's ready to leave
what it's always known.
To embark on the story being written
in a small house in Denver
that doesn't know me well but wants to,
as it teaches me how to fly.

My Dreams Live in Santorini

I have dreams,
as most of us do,
but mine don't live in my head or my heart,
they live somewhere on the shores of Santorini.

I think there are secrets hidden there,
of course I don't know what they are,
that's the nature of a secret.
But I believe life's greatest mysteries are
waiting to be found on that coastline.

Beautiful identities and names and loves
in those waves, not visible to the human
eye but perhaps to the right soul.

Santorini is beautiful, sure, but I think
it might be crafted of magic.
I want to swim in those waters
and maybe then my dreams will come alive.

What I'd Say

What would I say to you.
If I saw you in the street,
or in a coffee shop,
maybe waiting for the bus in the rain.

All the things I never told you,
that I've wanted to say for years.
Tell you that you never left my mind.
Tell you that you were the love that I lost.

I suppressed those feelings long ago,
because some things will just never come to fruition.
But I always had to wonder
what you would say,

if you had only known.

Organ Donor

I am a registered organ donor.
If I die and my body isn't strong enough
to hold my soul anymore,
the pieces of me that made up my existence contribute to
someone else continuing theirs.
I am a registered organ donor,
represented by the orange dot on my driver's license.

But I'm also an organ trader.
I give my heart away on the black market
without anyone being the wiser.
I shatter my ribs to reach into it's cage
and pull my heavy heart out
for anyone who needs it, in exchange
for a cheap love that leaves
quicker than their new heart can beat.

It's a good return on investment, I say.
I give them what they need now, and
someday they will recognize
the selflessness of giving them a vital organ.
Someday they will feel warmth of my heart in their chest.
Someday they will love me because I gave
the best parts of myself to them.

But that's the nature of being an organ donor.
You don't get them back. You're dead.
They slowly kill me until I too need a
donor.

Geyser.

I feel words bubbling up inside of me like a geyser
full of existential dread and it's going to

burst

at any moment and take out anyone in its path because
I can't hold these emotions anymore

and I can't pretend that I understand geologic time
but it feels like an

eruption

is long overdue and that I should take cover
because eventually it's all just going to

detonate.

To the One I've Hurt the Most

I hurt you.
And I know you say it's fine and that it's not my fault,
but it is.

Sure, I didn't manufacture their actions,
but I put both of us at risk
by even letting them in in the first place.

I wish there was something I could say to mend pieces
and tie up loose ends, but really,
the only thing we can do is wait for the wounds to scar.

Wait for the pain to subside,
and try better next time.
But I'm still sorry.

I'm sorry, my heart,
to have put you through it again.
I don't know how you still pump love in my veins.

When I've given you every reason to block the arteries,
and wait till I was really ready.
But I think we grew together.

I think we both got better, and it doesn't negate the pain
I put you through, but I think, if anything,
we might know how to love a little better next time,
even if we hurt again.

Walls

You taught me to build walls instead of bridges,

because some lives are never supposed to cross.

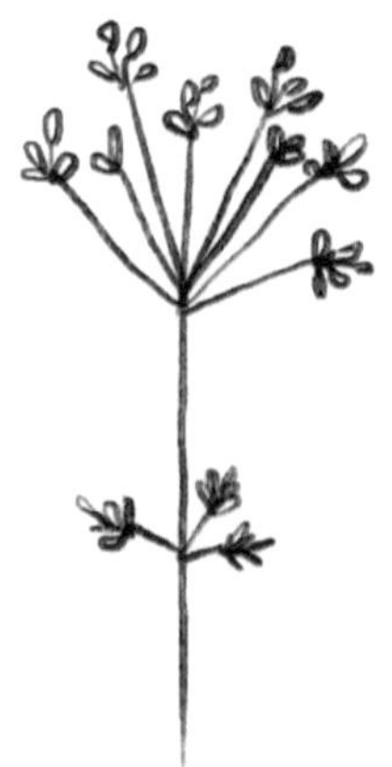

If I Found the Sky

An expanse so vast,
that only the horizon could contain it.
A blue so brilliant,
that even the ocean had to steal its hue.

Spotted with dots like freckles,
in mix-matched,
yet perfectly aligned fashion,
that can illuminate even the darkest night.

It's immensity the perfect company
to look up and admire
on a checkered blanket,
immersed in a lukewarm summer day.

Balloons filled with fire
can't help but dance in its magnitude,
and birds ride in its clouds,
on the migration towards home.

We have been abundantly blessed
with a blanket of sapphire,
that is one of the only constants in this life,
that you can look up to and adore.

Somewhere Along the Way I Learned How to Fly

That was the moment I knew I was better.
Maybe not healed, but better.

The wounds that would have left scars before,
didn't even draw blood.

The sad songs didn't resonate with me like they used to.

The moon wasn't my sound wall anymore,
and the sun became my friend.

I found a key hidden in plain sight,
when I was too busy looking in all
the wrong places of myself.

In the darkness,
in the loneliness,
the hurt,
the anger,

but it turns out, healing isn't found there.

Healing isn't found in the places we insist on staying,
it's found in the hard-to-reach places
that only the light can see.

I held the key all along,
and I finally unlocked the shackles from my wings,

and now I'm free to fly.

I Fell in Love and Made Them Homes.

Today I fell in love. I fell in love with the words on a page
that only the most agonizing experiences could write.
Words that made homes for people
who didn't deserve them.

Their name never spelled out, but the pain they caused
was burned into leather bound sheets
that cut as sharp as a kitchen knife.
The words I couldn't say without them
feeling remorse for their actions.

But why couldn't they know the cuts they made?
I built them perfectly good homes
made from sturdy enough wood
that went through years of refinement
to be told it wasn't good enough.

I had to spare their feelings, when they
so blatantly disregarded mine.
They took blueprints I had strategically crafted for them
and put them in the sink and let the ink
run like mascara down my cheeks.

Today I fell in love with a feeling so
excruciating that only it could construct
towers on such shaky ground that fall with a
closed door of a house they never wanted,

But I built for them anyway.

Past Tense

I changed know to knew,

and feel to felt

and love to loved,

because you're in the past now.

It means that I'm finally free

of whom you were,

and I get to know, feel, and love,

without it being about you.

Past tense.

I Feel Like a Toy

I feel like a toy.
Like I'm good for nothing,
except looking pretty and staying silent.

You may see me in the window of a toy store,
smiling a forced half open smile,
hoping that I will be enough for someone to pick me,

wrap me up with a bow,
take me home,
just to say they wanted a toy that they
could decide the actions of,

like an action figure or a barbie,
not of a 20-something woman that prefers
to keep some things to herself.
I don't want to just be their playground.

But that's the female condition, right?
Be who they want you to be,
be their toy?

Hindsight

I know it now, in *hindsight,*
that words and intention mean so *little* without
any action to back them up.

I know it now, in *hindsight,*
that some people never learned how to properly love,
at no fault of their own, and that fact has nothing to do
with me or my ability to *be* loved.

I know it now, in *hindsight,*
that you can't will someone into loving you,
and you can't expect *yourself* to be able to, either.

I know it now, in *hindsight,*
that we would have never been able to
co-exist, or *ebb and flow*, or *push and pull*
and maybe one or the other but certainly
not both simultaneously.

I know it now, in *hindsight.*
I just wish I had the *foresight* to know it *then.*

If Anxiety Had a Name

I used to be nothing more than an evolutionary trait
to protect people from snakes, spiders,
and all that is imminent danger.

But now I linger in the dark at 2am grieving my name
becoming a diagnosis in a 947-page book.

Squished between traumas and melancholia,
bipolar, and schizophrenia,

and they make sure to tell you that
you are not your diagnosis,
you're not depressed,

you have depression.

You're not ocd,

you just live through its lens.

You're not anxious,

you have anxiety.

You have me, and the only way you
can get rid of me is medication
or therapy, if you succeed in this at all.

I just wanted to keep you alive,
but I fear that all I did,
was drain you of life.

Fire Dances in the Rain

It wasn't until the rain fell,
that she could feel free.
Like the ruins of the whirlwind
had settled in debris.

This storm was a fierce one,
but there's no battle she couldn't win.
You see, the lightning can't touch what's in her
it can only hit her skin.

The flames in her are unstoppable,
an ever-burning light.
To put them out would take a tsunami,
and even then, they would put up a fight.

It's not something that she was born with.
It's something she had to learn.
To show people who she was,
to finally get her turn.

Her mind was like a forest fire,
that no one could contain.
But everything's a little wilder,
when it dances in the rain.

Broken Can Be Beautiful

All she wanted
was someone to pick up the pieces,
and make a mosaic
out of the ruins.

A Feeling That Just Can't be Described

I've been trying to describe this feeling in my chest.
A weight so heavy that only sadness could be the culprit.

A sadness so deep that the mind can't
bare the heaviness on its own,
and the heart has to take some of the burden.

I realized that while I can't describe the feeling itself,

I can describe the way you would always
look over at me as you drove,
I'd roll my eyes but didn't really mind.

I can describe how my heart sank when
you laughed into my shoulder
and sat just an inch too close.

I can describe the times that you called me a queen,
until the war came, and you joined the rebellion.

I can describe how your height lined
up perfectly with mine
so that when I hugged you, my chin
rested so easily on your shoulder.

I can describe the night you taught me to
swing dance in your living room
and the feeling of your hands on mine.

I can describe how listening to Taylor
Swift in your Chevy Impala
made me think for a split second that
maybe my heart knew how to love.

So, maybe I can't describe the feeling
itself, but I think that's pretty close.

Piano Keys

I never thought I'd be envious of piano keys,
or guitar strings.

But I found myself jealous
of how they would feel your touch,

in a way I never will.

I'm Not Worth the Wait

He said I wasn't worth the wait,
but that he would love to take me on a date.

That would inevitably end with him
wanting more than I was willing to give.

He said I was like the other girls that,
God forbid, made a decision about their own body,

that he didn't agree with.
He thought he had the rights to it.

He said he wouldn't be able to change his mind,
after I already said I wouldn't be able to change mine.

As if I had to compromise who I am
to fit the mold of who he wanted me to be.

I told him it made me uncomfortable
while he turned it all back on me.

And somehow made me feel like
I had to give up the deed
to the body I call my home just to be loved.

I know it's not all men. But it's hard
to keep that perspective
when all I get are men that tell me

I'm not worth the wait.

Where am I Supposed to Look?

"You'll find the one" they said
I did, but I held on too tight, and he loosened his grip.

"You'll find the one" they said
I did, but I fell too hard before he committed to holding
the safety net.

"You'll find the one" they said
I did, but our window of opportunity slammed shut
on my unsuspecting hands.

"You'll find the one" they said
I did, but he's gone. And now where
am I supposed to look?

How do you Describe Anxiety?

How do you describe a *feeling*
that doesn't *feel*
like a *feeling* at all,
but more of a state of being?

Numb.

How can you illustrate that you
are *feeling* everything at once,
but at the same moment *feeling*
absolutely nothing at all?
Like it's a blank canvas waiting to be

Ruined.

How should you explain to someone
feeling the pressure of a submarine?
Safe at 1000ft below the surface,
until one wrong move and water rushes in.

Submerged.

How would you represent
the demons in a mind that
point to the dictionary definition of *feeling*
that only give synonyms similar to that of
Love?

How do you comprehend this idea?
When all you feel is

<Numb>
<Ruined>
<Submerged>

and anything but

<Love.>

Hollow

It's the things that never seem to happen that carve out
pockets of hope for the next time and the next time
but those small divots at some point
become a gaping hole
that hollows out a heart until it can't
feel anything. Let alone hope.

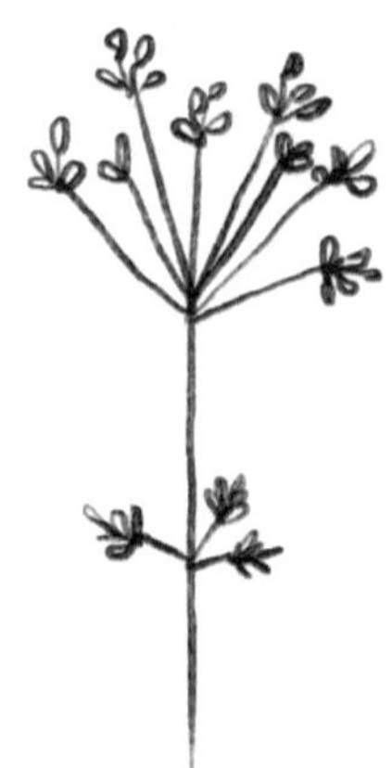

If I Wrote a Love Letter to New York

If I wrote a letter
to my first true love,
it would be mailed to zip code 10001.
It would travel some 1200 miles,
to get to the middle of a city
that never slows down long enough to read.
But I'd still write to it anyway.
I'd write about the magic on the street corners,
and the dreams in the alley ways.
The noise that is deafening enough
to make the world seem silent.
You can see the desire in the hearts of
dreamers who knew no other city
could contain the ambitions of thousands
of people waiting for a chance in the limelight.
The energies vibrate to a perfectly
choreographed melody
that is played in every taxi, on every street.
A city that takes up 302.6 mi^2 of space
and has never once apologized for it.
I see myself in you, New York.
Thank you for letting me in on your glamour,
if only for a little while.

Hurt and Heal

So, let it hurt.

Let it keep you up till 3am looking out the window
at the smokestacks on the neighboring roof.

Let it hurt.

Let it rip your heart open every morning and try to
stitch it back together throughout the day,
just for the same fate tomorrow.

Let it hurt.

Let it make some songs so unbearable to listen to
because every word is about him.

Let it hurt.

And then, after some time, let it heal.

Let it heal because you deserve more
than someone that keeps you at arm's length.

Let it heal because someone, someday is going to
know you fully and still love all the broken pieces.

And someday, when your heart has healed,
He will realize that letting you go was
the grandest mistake he could have made.

Let it hurt him,
let it heal you.

Wounds

I have wounds,
Bruises surfaced from stones
made of words that say one thing,
and actions that do another
The welts on my back weren't
from contact, but a
disappointment from within
I have metaphorical scars
so deep they will never heal
No medication or therapy can
take them away from the
forefront of a brain, ready to battle
waiting,
waiting at the frontline
for a chance to be set free
But there are some enemies
that need to be defeated
These enemies live submerged
in a conscious that simply wants
a chance to breathe
without being pelted
with fresh wounds

I'll Buy Myself Flowers

There's a vase my grandma gave
me that my grandpa filled
with lilies and roses every Saturday morning.

My grandma handed me the vase and asked me about the
men in my life. I had to regrettably
tell her there were none.

"Boys don't like me" I told her. "I'm too much for them.
I can't be put in a box like flowers in a
vase. I need room to bloom."

She nodded as if she could relate. She told
me to take the vase and give it time.

The vase has sat in my cupboard for years, collecting dust
and anything but petals. But today I filled it.

I filled it with flowers from a farmers
market that I bought for myself.
The prettiest lilacs I had ever seen.

I filled the vase with my own love,
because his soil wasn't fertile enough
to foster the love I deserved.

That vase is overflowing with flowers that
didn't need to come from a man.

Because I can love me,
even if he doesn't.

You Can't Leave Yet

You can't leave yet.
You have too many sunsets to watch,
lightning bugs to catch,
and trees to climb.
You can't leave yet.
You haven't seen all the corners of the world,
or smelt the fragrance of every flower.
You have yet to scale a mountain,
or step foot in every ocean.
You have so many songs to listen to
that haven't even been written yet,
and too many hands to hold to say goodbye now.

You can't leave yet.
So, stay.

ER

Why would he want to try so hard for me
when he could find someone easier,
someone less broken than I.

The shards of my being make others bleed
when they attempt to piece me together.
My fingers are calloused and used to the lesions,
but others don't know how to handle with care.

I'm a guaranteed ER visit of a person
because I always end up
leaving them with scars and bruises that
therapists don't know what to do with.

Wrap me in caution tape and words of
affirmation because I'm difficult.
I come with an emergency exit plan for easy escape
because that's what they need when they
go against doctor recommendation
and take a risk with me.

My heart is an ambulance that always
drives them to the hospital
to repair the damage I've caused. I'm a
shiny scalpel that looks sterile
until they sever a vital organ and
infection runs through their veins
and they end up in an ER bed next to all the others

That I drove away with my brokenness.

Addiction

And maybe I'm addicted to the pain.
Maybe I live for the low levels of serotonin,
and get high on heart break.

Maybe my addictive genes manifested
in despondence and dejection.
Dependency on tragedy.

An aversion to contentment,
an addiction to the darkness.

Incomprehensible

It's one of those feelings
so incomprehensible
that when you try to
explain it to someone,
the words escape you, or
perhaps they don't even exist.

This feeling has been the muse
for my words these days.
I've been searching for
metaphors to describe a pain
this profound, but nothing
seems to do it justice.

It's like there's a bird
pecking at your chest,
as if you're nothing
more than a carcass.
Constantly chipping
away at foundation until
the heart implodes.

And once it does, that's
where the weight comes in.
A weight that fills up
the entire ribs,
and puts immense
pressure on the lungs.
Breathing becomes
a challenge too.

It's like when the heart
finally gives, it sends a
tidal wave of brokenness
through every artery until
it simply consumes you.
And you sit.

You sit among the
shattered pieces,
all dripping in a fine
layer of crimson
as your lungs try to inflate to
keep at least one organ alive.
The pain seems so
existential. Inescapable.

You sit, and you take it.
You sit, and you feel it.

You let that bird sit on
your shoulder and sing the
songs that hurt the most.

But luckily, the body is
brilliant at repairing what
was almost too far gone.
It will sew up the veins,
and reassemble every rib.

It can take that splintered
heart and slowly start
to remind it how
the love it contains is just too
vast for some people to hold.
So, they drop it.

But you can pick it back up.
You pick it back up
because you have to.
And what was almost
too far gone,
just turns back into this feeling.
A feeling that is
incomprehensible.

Peace in the Thick of Things

In this small moment, too short to grasp,
I feel a fleeting peace in my soul.
I know it will leave soon, but for just this second, I feel ok.

I live for these moments because even
here in the thick of it all,
serenity can still be found in the dark places
at 12:30am when the world is asleep.

But I'm here awake with a heart that still beats,
and lungs that still breathe, and I think
that's a whole lot of magic.

Hurt You

You said you could never be in love again,
so that no one could hurt you.

But the things is,

you never gave me a chance not to.

The 20 Springs I've Seen

I've seen 20 springs now.
20 times I've seen the grass turn green,
I've seen the trees blossom,
and the weather slowly warm up until
we say screw it and wear
shorts in 50 degrees.

I've seen the relief on faces when the
darkness doesn't arrive quite so early,
and the snow diminishes into the soil.

I've seen 20 springs,
but none quite like this one.
This one feels a little lighter,
a little calmer,
a little quieter.

This spring feels like a rebirth of who
I was always meant to be.

I was hidden under ice caps and a frozen over lake,
and I got really good at holding my breath.
I got really good at morphing myself into
how the spring wanted me to grow.

But in my 20th spring,
I'm relearning how to breathe again.
I'm learning how to breathe without gasping for air
in fear of all the oxygen dissipating into the nothingness
that used to be every spring prior.

The nothingness was fertile soil all along.

So, thank you spring.
Thank you for a chance to begin again,
for the 20th time.

Rose Colored Glasses

If my glasses are rose tinted, let it be.

I can't help but look at you with a hopeful hue.

In My Dreams

My subconscious has a habit of
releasing all the thoughts I don't let
myself think during the day,
in a hurricane of sentiments
that come alive in the dead of night.

I imagine my eyelids flutter,
and I'm sure a soft smile
finds its way across my lips.
I can't even imagine the serotonin produced.
I suppose you have to get it somehow.

I'm someone different there.
All the rougher edges are sanded down,
the fragments of my being are laced
together with gold,
instead of being scattered on the floor.

The version of me that my subconscious
thinks I am is a lot stronger.
She's probably kinder,
probably prettier too.
No wonder you love her more than me.

In my dreams you love me,
or whoever it is I am there.
But that's why we sleep right?
To live the reality we wish we lived
when we're awake?

Keep Singing

The most comfort I have found in a while
was that of chirping at 7am in a city that was
-15° and had barely a hint of sun.

But the birds still sang.

It's Just a Yellow Ball.

It was the most crystal-clear blue sky I had
seen since before the turmoil. Not because
there hadn't been any, I just hadn't look up
from the ground long enough to notice.

The daycare across the street had a constant chatter
that almost turns itself into a white noise machine,
and you notice the silence more than the sound.

There was a yellow ball resting on the sidewalk that
found its way past the enclosure that housed the magic
that are kids. Not because they have any supernatural
powers, but because they still have the capability to
dream. What so many of us lost at an early age.

I sat on this patio with my notebooks and pens hoping
that the formulas and calculations would lead me to
fulfillment. That if I can just get through this physics
class, I can accomplish the "dreams" I set out to find.

A little girl in a pink floral print dress stood at the edge
of the fence with a small arm through the wire, reaching
for the yellow ball that fell on the sidewalk below.

I understood that feeling. Being so far out of
reach from what you want most and being stuck
in a cage of normalcy with no room for becoming
much more than what you already were.

I walked across the street and picked up the ball
to hand to her. I gave her back what she wanted,
and for myself, perhaps I should do the same.

My Seasons

Every time the thunder sounds,
my heart cries out for you.
The voices in my head
are getting louder,
I hope you can hear them too.

The night is dark
and cloudy now,
but you're my guiding star.
Yet every time the
lightning bolts,
it leaves me with a scar.

I want so badly to witness
the sunrise before I quit.
Even though I'm meant for you,
sometimes things don't always fit.

Like rain on a day of sun,
or snow in mid-July,
I hope you see the
seasons in me,
before we both may die.

I'm made up of many things,
the seasons are among a few.
I'm the raging thunder
in the spring,
and the blooming flowers too.

I'm the summer sun that's shining,
and the blizzard on the roof.
The leaves that
slowly fall down
are my only source of proof.

You don't know my
seasons though,

you didn't take the time
to know my mountains
and boulders,
that you were too
weak to climb.

You know the darker edges.
The storm on the deadly sea.
But what you forgot to look for,
were the better parts of me.

The greeting morning sun
as it gently kisses your skin,
or the sweet breeze
on a blazing day,
see, you don't know
where I've been.

I have seen the cycle
many times,
winter, spring,
summer, and fall.
You don't see these in me,
because you don't know me at all.

There are still parts of me
that I have yet to find.
You will look for me
in other women,
but I am one of a kind.

You can search for many miles,
but it won't be me you'll see.
Because even with
billions of people,
there aren't any more
seasons like me.

Wishful Thinking

And when you know me,
I hope you don't run.
I hope my baggage makes you hold my hand tighter.
I hope you wrap your arms around me from behind,
and tell me "I'm never letting go."
I hope you see my scars as abstract art,
and not an impossible game of connect the dots.
I hope you put your coat around me when I'm cold,
and blow warm air on my poorly circulated hands.
I hope you ease my tangled mind with reassuring words,
even if you have to promise you love me twice a day.
I hope you love me how I need to be loved.
But that is all just
wishful thinking.

Hello, 2:00 a.m.

Hello, moon in the distance:
my only company at this hour,
a tender light that shines,
but never seems to burn.
Nothing can ignite flames of doubt now-
except my eyes,
after being engulfed in salty waves.
Not even the moon can control these tides.

Hello, stars scattered above me:
They seem so disordered,
yet don't ask to be sewn together in patter.
So perfectly dispersed,
without a needle and thread in sight.
Each one like a memory
that stiches itself into my brain on this late night,
I always analyze the things I wish I could change.
There are no shooting stars tonight.

Hello, darkness around me:
a navy cast amongst the world,
more beautiful than the day.
A reminder that not everything is always bright.
Sometimes darkness is the only way
to see the light.

It Was More Than a Parking Receipt

It was nothing more than a parking receipt.
A dollar for 2 hours,
September 4, 2020,
at 11:21am.
Space 1621,
downtown Minneapolis.

It was nothing more than a parking receipt.
But when I took it out of my wallet,
and hovered it over the garbage,
ready to release,
I couldn't let go of it.

Because that day it was more than a parking receipt.
At that time,
that parking space,
your moms red van because your car was in the shop
after you rear ended someone,
that was more than just a day.

That was more than a parking receipt,
and more than just an ordinary September 4th at 11:21am.

This was the day
I fell in love with you.
Forever commemorated,
in nothing more
than a wrinkled up
parking receipt.

We Write About What Hurts

I'm not sure why I always fall for boys I can't have.

Maybe it's because they always make for the

best poetry.

Every Time, All the Time

Every time I think of you my heart feels heavy,
I wonder if you'll ever leave this home
you made inside my heart.

Every time I remember us, and I forget to breathe,
I can't help but think if I ever cross your mind.

Every time I think you're gone, and I
can open my heart up again,
your image stares me right in the face.

It reminds me that after all this time,
it's still you.

Every time,

and

all the time.

Wild in Her Veins

There was wild that lived inside of her,
that only he knew.
Rivers flowed so effortlessly through her veins.
Her love ran deeper than the Dead Sea.

She couldn't see this, though.
Her wings had been clipped,
her spirit trampled by those
who were threatened by her magic.

She calmed her ocean of a mind
to make a safe home for row boats,
where there should have only been
the strongest ships on the sea.

She couldn't let the lions roar,
scared of what they all may think.
But he wasn't afraid of her strength,
he wanted to dance with it.

Fields of dandelions took up most of her heart,
all he wanted to do was make one wish.
That she wouldn't be afraid of her power,
but that she would embrace it.

Like the sun radiating against your face,
after a frigid winter day.

For You

I hoped that one day,
if these words got pressed between bound pages
and were released into the world,
you would pass by a bookstore,
look in the window,
and my name on the cover would be a distant memory.

You would open to the first page and see
that all these words were written

just for you.

Laying in the Loneliness

Laying in the same spot,
in the same solitude,
with the same music playing
as when I was 15 is a surreal thing.

It's like nothing has changed,
yet absolutely nothing has stayed the same.
not my heart, not my standards, not my life,
and not me.

But as I lay here,
in the room that I first put pencil to paper,
I can't help but wonder why, after
everything has changed,
the loneliness never did.

The loneliness still strangles my lungs
with every inhale,
and makes my chest ache
just the same as it always did.

Maybe there are some things we just can't escape.
No matter how many years pass us by.

So, I guess I'll lay here
in a feeling too complex to name.
Loneliness in its purest form,
isolated from the things my heart always craved,

but never came close to.
The closest I came was laying in an
empty room hoping somewhere
in the world there would be another person
well acquainted with the same feeling.

Someone that would someday
lay in the loneliness
with me.

Wings

Allow the cinderblocks
on your shoulders to turn to
feathers

These feathers will become your
wings.

A Poem for Josh: Someday, Soon.

Someday all the problems of this moment will
diminish into the slowly setting sun.

The moon will rise in the sky to remind us
that beauty also lives in the dark.

Winter won't feel so heavy,
spring will feel light again.

Your heart will dance with the dandelions,
and you won't need to wish for a single thing.
You'll already have it.

When day turns to night and collapses into
the horizon, you won't have to
fear your mind anymore.

You can drift off to sleep with someone you love,
and someone can always be yourself.

Someday soon, everything will be well.
Someday soon, your heart will love again.
Someday soon, it will all be worth it.

And I live for the magic in "Someday."

Recollections

I am very attached to my trauma.
It's almost like all the memories
burned into my brain, like branding of leather, can finally
serve some sort of purpose.

I gather them into a box labeled
"Recollections I can't touch",
and hide them away in my subconscious,
letting them manifest as they wish.

They show themselves in running
back to suffering's safety,
every time joy creeps a little too close.

And in abandoning people before they
have the chance to leave me.

And in therapy sessions when they
tie my tongue with wire,
and won't let me tell their tale, otherwise I
might be able to move on without them.

I can scream into oblivion all the lies they
force fed me, but what's the use?

No matter what medication or treatment I throw at them,
they always edge their way back into
the crevices of my mind
that had finally seen the light, just to blow it out.

So instead of ridding myself of them, I became attached.
Like they were my favorite chapter of
the most traumatic book my life could have written.

Used to Be

 My heart is beating fas-

No

Palpating.

My brain feels like a 90s
rainbow tie dye swirl and
at the eye of the cyclone is
an inevitable end that

goes

D
  O
    W
      N

and never stops because a
constant free fall without
a branch to grab on to
or a ledge to land on is
all my body knows.

Legs are unsteady,
wobbly, uneasy.

Stomach is like an endless
spin cycle that can only stop
with reassurance and losing
consciousness to dream land,

because it's there
that it all stops

STOPS.

Like I can press pause in reality,
like watching every car halt to
a stop at a red light that they
thought they could make.

I thought I could make it stop
with rationale and reason

but the only tools in my tool
kit vanish at the sight of fear.

I'm left in an open field all

Alone

With pre-thunder storm winds
barreling right through me
as if I weren't a person but
a ghost of someone who

Used

             To

    Be.

13-to-20

I was a 13-year-old girl,
so excited to sit around a pile of pillows,
and stay up until midnight talking about
all the boys that we wanted to have.

And now, I'm a 20-year-old girl,
terrified of love and
staying up till 3am with tears in my pillow
thinking about all the boys that broke my heart.

Like I Did

Every time you find someone new
that isn't me,
I file through her pictures
and anything I can to compare myself to her.

A girl who doesn't know me,
a girl who doesn't know how you hurt me.
She's lucky,
I wish I were her.

I don't know her,
I don't know anything more than her name.
But the envy I have for her chance to love you
is consuming my mind.

I hope she knows she's lucky.
I hope you tell her all the things you reluctantly told me,
trying to protect your tough image,
that I saw right through.

I hope she sees through it.
I hope she can see the you that hides
behind manufactured
joy and robotic laughs.
Because you need that.

You need someone that understands you,
and is more in love with who you are
than who you pretend to be.
I hope she loves you.

I hope she loves you like I did.

They Always Leave Me Nothing

You went from being one of the most important

people in my life,

to being barely anything at all.

That seems to be a pattern for me.

I pour my heart into people that decide they want to leave,

and they take my love with them.

Just "be"

I don't know how to just "be".
And that to me is terrifying,
because what if there comes a time
that I'm not chasing a dream,
and I have to sit still, which seems
like planting roots in one place,
and I've never been good at that.
Because I like to wander and, in this case,
I can't stray too far from home
because my identity lives there, but my soul is a nomad.
My soul is a weary traveler looking for an inn
but they say she occupies too much space.

I don't know how to just "be".
And that makes me nervous
because what if I'm always looking
ahead to the horizon without seeing what's right under my feet.
What if I'm looking for fulfillment in islands and
peninsulas that require a lifetime of swimming and
staying afloat just to find that what I was searching
for lived closer to me than I could have imagined.
 I just never looked at the ground long enough to see it.

I don't know how to just "be".
And I'm starting to see
that this may be a problem because I'm always running,
and at some point, my endurance will fall short.
I will collapse, and my lungs won't inflate, and my
heart will stop beating, and I'll be laying in dirt forced
to be nothing more than a corpse. I want to learn
how to just "be" before there's nothing left of me.

I want to learn to just "be" before I
look back on my life and see
that I only ever sprinted and never enjoyed the scenery.

I want to just "be" before that's my
only
option
left.

I Love the Night

I'm much prettier in the dark.
You can't see the purple lines
that run across my pelvic bone.

I'm much prettier in the dark.
The dots that scatter my face
are practically invisible.

I'm much prettier in the dark.
My pale complexion just looks like
another shade of skin.

I'm much prettier in the dark.
Maybe that's why
I love the night.

Someday I Will

I don't know who you are yet.

I can't imagine that our paths have already crossed
in any other circumstance than
strangers sitting on bus seats
or passing by on the street.

I don't know what your name is yet.
I always loved the name Will.
I used it as a filler name in all of my
stories I wrote as a child.

Maybe they were about you all along.

I don't know your scars yet.
Do you wrap them in books and songs?
Or in bottles of empty tequila?

Those bottles generally only make for more band aids.

I don't even know your favorite color yet.
It's an essential first question.
You can tell a lot about a person by if their favorite color
is gray or blue.

Mine has always been yellow.

I don't know who you are,
or when I will get to meet you.
I don't know any of these answers yet.

But someday, I will.

A Heartbroken Afternoon on a Tuesday at 3

He didn't mean to, I don't presume,
but he somehow controlled my heart like a marionette.

      He directed my feelings like a puppet on strings.
      And I let him, because what else was I to do?

What other choice did I really have
besides believing his words and quixotic declarations?

      His words were extravagant,
followed by little action,
      but I believed him all the same.

I believed him because I didn't know
how to accept real love,
so, I settled for love that was just another Tuesday.

      I settled for love that was a frequent visitor
      dressed as heartbreak, on a Tuesday at 3.

A Large House on 28th Street

There's a big tan house on the corner
of 28th and Emerson.

It's not glamorous, probably built in the 70s.
Popcorn rolled paint on the exterior with dark wood trim.
White columns with a wraparound porch.

I have passed this house many times.
It's truly not that special.
I never noticed it until I looked out the window of the car,
sitting next to someone I once loved,
and saw it for more than a house.

Something about it made me want to live.
Something about it made me want to see my future
because maybe I'll have a house like that someday.

So now, it serves as a reminder.
A reminder that someday things might be different.
Someday might be wonderful,
and I might live in a very average house
in an average part of town
living an extraordinary life.
And all I have to do is keep living to
find out.

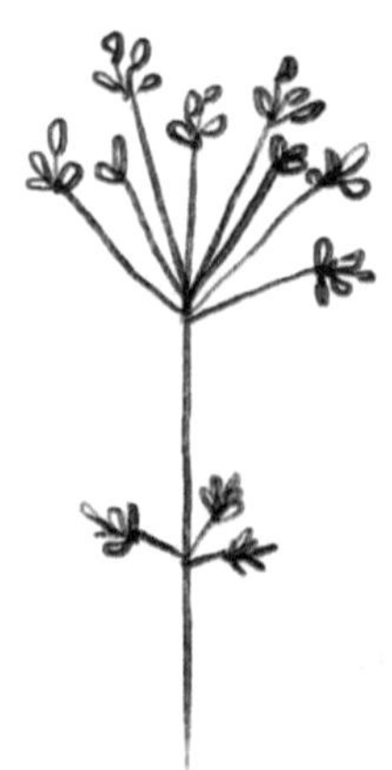

Lions

My hands were bound,
my mouth sewed shut.

Dressed in remains of my youth
with regret dripping through the fibers.

Draped in bubble wrap and trauma
and nestled in a box to keep me quiet.
But they can't silence a voice that screams
far over the mountain tops.

That stops the oceans in its path
because it's scared to get in the way.

That runs wild with the lions,
not afraid of what is over the hill.

They thought they could break me.

But they can't break a heart that was made to

roar.

Beat Them to the Punch

Leave them before they leave you.

Find something wrong with them
before they see something wrong in you.

Deceive them before they deceive you,
hate them before they hate you,
run before you give them a chance to.

Beat them to the punch.

Crying, Cribbage, and Corduroy

I have only played the game once.
I barely listened to the instructions,
as I battled the intermittent aches in my chest
while I smeared mascara all around my eyes.

It was a cold day in January,
and all I remember is feeling like
my sternum was being split
in two with a dull blade and my heart
being compact by a hydraulic press.

I hadn't seen the game since.
Until today.
Today it was a beautiful mahogany board
with 360 holes and 3 different colored pegs.

My heart hadn't felt that gut-wrenching feeling since.
Until today. Today it was a camel
colored corduroy button up
with the stretched-out neckline of a white
t-shirt from where the guitar strap liked to tug.

I thought I was fine, but
today it was card tricks,
and the most recognizable laugh.
Today it was his smile that turns
his eyes into crescent moons,
and his shoes that are never tied.

Today it was the same ache
that has lingered for months now.
Triggered by the most random of things.
Crying, cribbage, and corduroy.

If Only

The pain resurfaced the second I saw you look
at me with those eyes I could drown in.

If only you had let me swim.

I could see the sheer hopelessness on your
face when you told me you were lonely.

If only I had been there.

The well sorted rationalizations of why we
would never work started to dismantle themselves.

If only we could have tried.

And we sat there, so desperate to feel anything in a world
that makes you believe no one will ever really care.

But I did.

And you could have too.

If only you had loved me.

Closer

I don't know who you are,
where you are,
or when I'll get to meet you.

But tonight,
we rest under the same stars,
the same moon,
and with the same intention of falling in love someday.

And tomorrow we will wake up to the same sun,
and it will remind me
that even on the worst days,
there is always a new beginning on the morning horizon.

These truths make it feel like you're not so far away.
As long as we look up and see the same sky,
I'm closer to you in this universe
than a million miles apart.

It's Just a Season

Everything has a season,

this one just happens to be dark by 4pm and the sun sets
before the rays can even touch my skin.

Just One.

You asked me if I had any questions,
after I told you all the things you did wrong.
Politely asking if there was any more
that could possibly be addressed,
as if all the words I said didn't sum it up well enough.

You asked me if I had any questions,
while you held back tears, and your
eyes were glossed over.
Right after you told me how much I had meant to you,
how close you had felt to me.

You asked me if I had any questions,
while I sat there trying to hold on to any of the progress
my heart had made, with tears streaming down my face.

I did have a question.
I didn't ask it though,
because I didn't want to break my
own heart with the answer.

Just one question.

Why wasn't I enough?

The Most Broken Man I've Met

We're all a little broken,
a little crazy,
maybe a little mad.

We all have stories that never escape our mouths,
and strait jackets around the most
vulnerable pieces of our history,
while fabricating the mess.

We all hide some skeletons,
however, I've met some a little more tattered than the rest.

Some a little more shattered, a little more scattered,
a little more afraid of their past.

I met a man who was lost on a fog-stricken path,
with no visibility of the hillcrest.

He didn't wear his heart on his sleeve,
it protruded right from his chest.

He felt so much,
thought so much,
and was never dishonest.

He was the most broken man I'd met.

But somehow, he made me feel just a little more

whole.

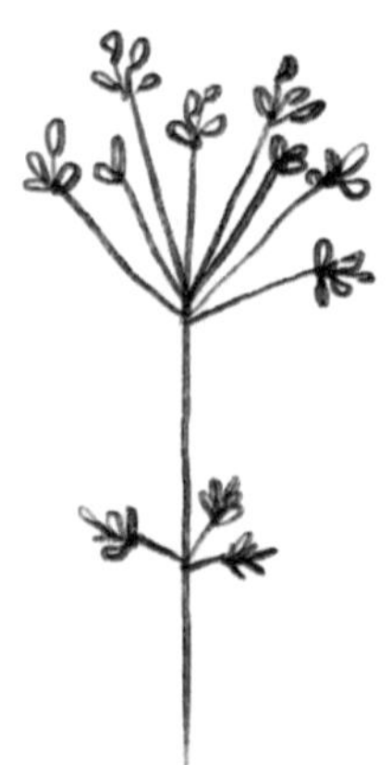

Ash

Missing you comes in phases
like the moon.
One day it's as small as a crescent,
and soon it's as vast as the tide.

Missing you comes in waves
like a tsunami.
One day it's smooth sailing,
The next it engulfs my eyes in salty tears.

Missing you comes in rays
like the sun.
One day it's covered by clouds,
the next it burns up what's left of me.

Missing you is hell.
I just hope someday,
my hell will feel less like raging fire,
and more like dying

ash.

Row Boats and Shades of Blue

My heart beats a little faster
when I see your sky-blue eyes.
They remind me of all the tears
that my ocean eyes have cried.

But the difference between these blue hues,
is what lies below the surface.
You have a box with 4 walls built,
and I have a fire burning with purpose.

You have a small row boat,
it gets you to the shore.
But what's the fun in playing it safe,
when there can be so much more?

There are Australian lakes that are pink,
and New York sky scrapers in the clouds.
There are bird species in Africa
that have yet to be found.

You can take your small boat,
and flow right down the river.
Or, you can live a little wilder,
and chase what gives you shivers.

The sea may be blue,
and the sky has its own shade too,
but the difference in these colors,
is the difference between me and you.

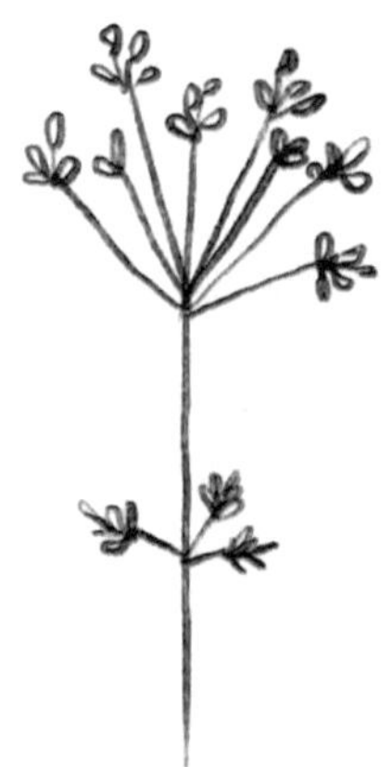

Você e Linda

He said he knew Portuguese,
and I told him to say something.

"Você e linda" He said.

"What does that mean?" I asked.

"Oh nothing" he replied.

"Você e linda" he says.

He said without knowing me, like they all do. They say
of a complexion that will wrinkle and hair that will
grey. Você e linda they say to an exterior so mortal.

"Você e linda" I whispered to my heart. To my soul,
to the eternal elements, to the things I wish made me
beautiful. To the pieces of me I fought hardest for
that live beyond the long blonde hair and blue eyes,
although I struggle to find those beautiful, too.

"Você e linda" I say.
"Você e linda".

And I'll live the rest of my life trying to believe it.

February

Some days I can't help but fall in love

with the fresh snow

on a heartbroken afternoon

in the cold February air.

I'm Afraid of my Own Words

There are words that I may be too afraid to write.
Words that carry too much pain and resentment.

Words that sprawl themselves out in my cerebrum
and make a home in my subconscious,
waiting for me to find them again someday.

Words that I repressed.
Words that left my tongue limp and
tied my vocal cords in knots.

If I can barely think about them, how
am I supposed to write them?
Exposed on lined paper dripping with ink and intention.

I begin to realize,
These were the exact words I needed to say.
These were the words that needed to be written.
These words are who I am,
but with that,
I suddenly began to fear
myself.

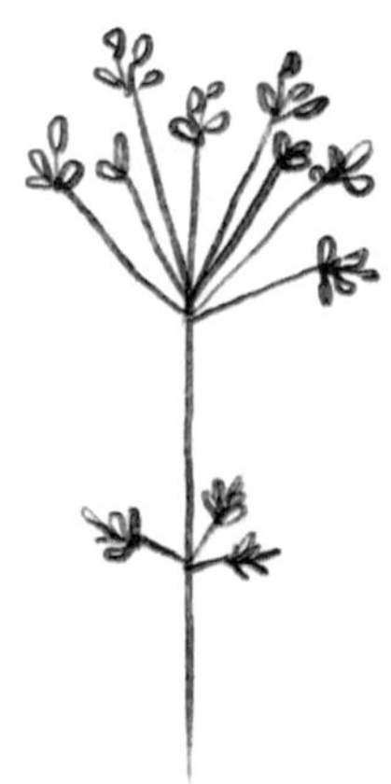

Stop and Breathe

I am well acquainted with disaster.
It's all my life has ever seen.
The sky is always gray,
and the grass is never green.

I'm scared of being complacent
because I have to prepare for the worst.
I can't just stop and breathe,
I have to write a survival guide first.

I don't know what my path looks like.
The twists and turns get in the way.
I can't stop racing to the finish line,
there's nowhere I can stay.

It's exhausting always running,
but that's what you learn to do
when everything around you crumbles
if you lose focus for a moment or two.

I've lived among the ruins,
building castles from the dust.
I've become quite the architect,
constructing a life made out of rust.

I'll know when I've reached it,
this place I'm meant to be.
I'll make a home from all the ashes,
just you wait and see.

Knew Better

And if I didn't know better
I'd let my childlike heart convince me to give it a try,
to see what happens.
It always tries to tell me that this could be the one,
and I might miss out
pushing me to take the leap.

But I do know better,
I've known better too long for my own good.
And that stops me from taking a chance with you.
Because this chance is 50/50,
and I think we would err on the side
that would end up with another broken heart
that simply
knew better.

Outlet

I could feel the spark between our hands,

like electricity surging through our fingertips.

How lovely it is to witness the tenderness

of a thousand fairy lights,

the mosaic of a million lit up Christmas trees,

and the false magic of a plane in the night sky.

It was as if the wires were finally aligned

to produce a sustainable current.

But the craftsmanship was faulty,

the circuits shorted,

 and not enough time dedicated to
perfectly bent conduits.

 It left us in the dark.

Someone had to pull the plug.

Blanket

You know when you take a freshly
washed blanket out of the dryer,
and it's so warm and soft that being wrapped in it
makes you feel safe and at home?

And it's not perfect, it has some loose threads,
maybe a stain here and there from wine nights,
or grass from the last picnic,

but it still serves its purpose, and does it well,
and you don't think anything differently
about its ability to be a good blanket,
even with a few imperfections.

That's how I want to feel.
That's what I think love should feel like.

Erasing History

You sharpen your sword like a pencil,
and acuminate the tip of your tongue
with words that don't leave cuts,
but traces of your signature all over, dripping in graphite.

You forget about me as you erase our past and
swipe away the debris likes there's nothing left of me
and nothing left of us.

I didn't know I was so forgettable, unmemorable,
but now I'm unrecognizable,
an idea that's become a crinkled up rough
draft, disposed of and neglected.

You can erase me,
but you can't erase our history.

Death Grip

I hold on tight,
my knuckles turning white like I'm
driving during a flash flood.

I hold on tight,
trying to cram as much of a first love
as I can into the short time
I will have with them before they leave.

I hold on tight,
holding back tears looking in the mirror
asking myself where I went wrong,
what I did wrong,
why I can't make them stay.

So, I flee before they can,
I crash the car before he does,
because the more miles traveled the
harder it is to say goodbye.

I have a collection of reasons for why
they weren't right for me anyway,
in attempt to nurse a heart covered in sheet metal to
convince myself that I'll be better off without them.

I hold on tight.

I hold on tight,
because fear of abandonment is always lingering,
and that's why I have such a
strong death grip.

A Door to an Empty Home

It's a strange thing to return home
after so much time spent away.

It doesn't quite feel the same.
Yes, the floor still creaks upstairs,
and the dryer makes as much noise as it always did.

But there are second nature habits
that become a mystery again.

Like which way the shower handle turns,
where each light switch connects to,
or how many seconds it takes for the microwave to heat up
the same oatmeal you used to eat every
day, before your time away.

Perhaps the most important habit broken
was believing the home was ever full.

The home is a house, and the family is just occupants
of a space labeled to mean some sort of connectedness
that it never seemed to find.

So no, it's not vacant, not empty of human life.
But it's empty of love, unoccupied by hope,
untenanted by laughter, clear of joy, deserted from entity.

That's part of growing up, I suppose,
learning these things that I was once
too young to understand.
But I've come to find that the nostalgia
knocks a little harder on the doors you don't open anymore.

Especially when they belong to that of an empty house.

Alternatively, Peace.

He told me to write about peace,
rather, how I've found it.
And to be quite honest,
I'm not sure that I have.

I'm beginning to think that peace is
not the addition of something,
or something to be discovered or uncovered.

But perhaps the ridding of shackles
that have a dense layer of rust from years of anchorage.

Chains disintegrating, flames turned to ash.

The disposal of doubt
and the resurrection of hope.

Maybe that's peace, maybes it's not.
And maybe I'll never find it.

Alternatively,
I may have found a pocket of peace with him,
at 11:30pm,
in an abandoned parking lot,
with a singular star in the sky.

Verdure

Every winter, the air pierces my face
like needles puncturing a pin cushion,
each gust biting a bit more than the last.

Days become shorter, spirits become lamented,
and the sun becomes a martyr under
the jurisdiction of glacial frost.

Perhaps that's not fair, because there can still be
magic amidst the bitter chill, but it's much harder to find
and I don't often have the impulse to perceive it.

But we know it doesn't end here.
The greatest dichotomy of them all
is that of winter to spring.
A display of perseverance, a picture of hope.

Green.
Green as far as the horizon allows.
Green touching every corner, met
with a rich shade of blue,
an incandescence that we almost
forget in the dead of winter.

It's new,
It's lively,
It's expectant,
It's verdure.

I dream of verdure,

I dream of the life to come.

ABOUT THE AUTHOR/ACKNOWLEDGEMENTS

Writing in third person has always felt weird to me, and if you read this book, I think we're on a first name basis at this point, I'll talk to you like a friend. My name is Kylie, I am 21 at the time of publishing this book, and I'm graduating from University of Minnesota this Spring (2022) with a degree in Biology and a minor in Public Health. Science is one of my loves, but writing was my first love. Writing is the only thing I was ever sure about my purpose being, transcribing what's in my heart on to thin lined paper. I started this journey at 15, given, everything I wrote at that time was awful, but with years and practice, I landed upon my voice. The more life I lived, the more I had to write about. The older I got, the more courage I had to uncover the things in my past that I couldn't bear to touch at 15. Courage to finally walk through the journey with God on how to accept what I couldn't change, courage to let Jesus move in my life.

I love doing outreach in inner cities, being on worship team, along with playing piano, singing, and writing music. Volleyball was ones of my first passions, and I love hiking with my dogs whom I adore.

I am so grateful to my friends that encouraged me in my writing, first thank you goes to Thana Zoske, my friend since the age of 3, who was the first person I ever let read my words. I am so thankful that she encouraged me to keep writing when I was a sophomore in high school, even though what I wrote then was awful, our brains were a little less developed than now. But needless to say, I wouldn't have become the writer I am if she hadn't encouraged me first.

Second goes to my therapist of almost 5 years, Anne. She has seen me in all my seasons and has encouraged me through them all. She believed in me, fought for me, and taught me how to fight for myself. I wouldn't be who I am without her help in the darkest times of my life.

Sydney Cashman, who is always the first one to receive a text of a new poem, and who has been with me through some of the worst times of my life. She has helped me in my faith immensely, and I'll never be able to thank her enough. I am so lucky to call her a best friend for life.

And finally, Kyri Rebholz, who has never been afraid to tell me when something didn't read right or didn't make sense or simply just sucked. Tough love, and I've needed that a time or two or hundred, in writing and in life. Another person I am so very thankful to have in my life as an editor, and a friend.

I have been abundantly blessed with the people in my life, and I am so lucky to have them. I'm so grateful to have made it this far, and for all the moments to come. Thank you for reading my book. Thank you for helping one of my dreams come true.

Follow my Instagram!
@words.by.kylie

www.ingramcontent.com/pod-product-compliance
Lightning Source LLC
Chambersburg PA
CBHW021353150726
47989CB00005B/2234